Fostering the Fire of Your Heart

Strength Through Christ
Devotional Anthology

Compiled by
Niki Barlow
Bobbie Bomar Brown

This book is dedicated to all of you who have known struggle, walked through trials, and carried the weight of your own fires. May these pages be a reminder that you are not alone. We pray that God opens your heart to receive what He has prepared for you within these words.

With deep gratitude, we thank the contributing authors
for sharing their voices and stories.

To our families and friends who have stood beside us during this journey, offering encouragement, love, and strength—thank you.

Contents

Thriving After the Fire | Niki Barlow 1

Truth in His Promises 3

Beyond the Waterfalls | Bobbie Bomar Brown 5

Cookies for God? | Bobbie Bomar Brown.. 7

Outskirts | Millie Carpenter... 9

Pinky Promises | Shelby Perryman 11

Trusting His Plan | Debra Hill-Gray 13

Unbreakable Promise | Bobbie Bomar Brown 15

Waiting | Jordan Ramos.. 17

When There's Nowhere to Go | Millie Carpenter........................... 19

Trust in God **21**

Enduring the Race | Niki Barlow... 23

The Flood | Trudy Hewitt... 25

Spiritual Drift | Greg Grandchamp 27

The Lord Shepherds Me | Katie Erickson..................................... 29

The Lord Restores and Protects Me | Katie Erickson..................... 31

The Lord Pursues Me | Katie Erickson 33

The Possibilities of the "What-Ifs" | Kirsten Wegele....................... 35

Worry or Trust? Our Choice | Greg Grandchamp 37

Fostering the Heart..**39**

A Smoldering Coal | Niki Barlow 41

Be Transformed | Millie Carpenter.. 43

Forgiveness | Greg Grandchamp.. 45

Love with Legs | Joe Pierce.. 47

Playing Frisbee | Trudy Hewitt.. 49

This Little Light of Mine | Debra Hill-Gray................................. 51

Those on Whom His Favor Rests | Karren Mitchell....................... 53

Wiped Clean | Joe Pierce 55

Stepping Into God's Presence..**57**

Divine Intervention | Jordan Ramos 59

Fearing the Unknown | Niki Barlow 61

Feasting Our Faith with Prayer | Greg Grandchamp 63

God Shows Up in Big Ways | Jordan Ramos 65

Prayer Rock | Trudy Hewitt 67

Pressing Past the Pain Into His Presence | Kirsten Wegele 69

Self-Reflection | Bobbie Bomar Brown...71

Teach the Children | Karren Mitchell 73

Beauty From Ashes.. **75**

Checking the Currency in Our Testimony | Kirsten Wegele 77

Forgiveness Not Returned | Joe Pierce 79

The Annunciation | Millie Carpenter 81

The Lord Is My Shepherd | Karren Mitchell..................................83

Till Death We Didn't Part… | Joe Pierce.......................................85

Turning Adversity Into Hope | Debra Hill-Gray............................87

Victory from Tragedy | Trudy Hewitt 89

When the Rivers Rage | Niki Barlow 91

Meet the Authors **93**

Thriving After the Fire

Niki Barlow

*"For my own name's sake I delay my wrath; for the sake of my
praise I hold it back from you, so as not to destroy you completely.
See, I have refined you, though not as silver; I have tested you in
the furnace of affliction."*
-Isaiah 48:9-10

Smoke billowed in the distance as the forest erupted into
flames, consuming 9,668 acres. How can anything good come from a
fire that devastates our land and destroys everything in its path? After
the vegetation burns, the land is renewed. The ashes of the burnt
organics release nitrogen and phosphorus, creating nutrient-rich soil
that enables fresh growth.

God created plants like lodgepole pine to restore the earth after
fire. Resin coats the cones, storing seeds for decades. The forest fire's
high heat melts the coating, releasing the seeds. Sometimes we become
stagnant or hide a sin for years. Trials come and God uses them to
burn the outer layers away, exposing what needs changed. He gives us a
pathway to an emerging life that often exceeds our expectations.

Fireweed, a beautiful flower, is among the first to grow in
burned areas. A single plant can produce up to 80,000 seeds per year,

1

which travel by wind. When we give our testimony, it speaks to others, encouraging them to come through the flames. Their changed lives affect those around them and generations to come.

Pinegrass burns quickly, but its roots live on, which allows the grass to regrow rapidly. It rarely blooms, but after a fire, it blooms for several years. Sometimes we may feel like our world is burning, but when we are rooted in Christ, He builds us up so we may bloom into a new creation.

Just as plant life thrives after forest fires, God uses the ashes in our lives to nurture fresh growth. Our hardships produce a stronger heart, mind, and faith. When going through struggles, we must rely on Him, which teaches us trust. God is our hope and salvation not because of our actions, but because of His.

The photo on the cover of this book was taken from my back porch during a forest fire. Several days later, scrolling through my pictures, I saw the perfect heart shining through the tree. I do not know how it got there, but it is a reminder of God's love for us through the flames and trials of this world. He uses fire to foster our hearts' growth, giving us the time to be renewed and redeemed.

God, create in us a new being, one more like Christ. Help us see what we need to change, and let our growth be seen by others to reflect You. When we are afflicted, be near us. Thank You for giving us the time and the desire to become so much more than we are today. Amen.

Truth in His Promises

Stand firm on God's promises, even when life is a struggle

Beyond the Waterfalls

Bobbie Bomar Brown

"Therefore, we do not lose heart. Though outwardly we are wasting away, yet inwardly we are being renewed day by day. For our light and momentary troubles are achieving for us an eternal glory that far outweighs them all. So we fix our eyes not on what is seen, but on what is unseen, since what is seen is temporary, but what is unseen is eternal."
-2 Corinthians 4:16-18

In the midst of downsizing, preparing to move into a smaller place, I can't help but reflect on my past homes. At a young age, I wanted "the" big house, justifying it would be my forever home. I have lost count of my dream homes. The excitement of purchasing new furniture and decorating the walls faded with each repeated process—packing, donating, moving, and redecorating.

Finally, I know the meaning of the term "forever home": It's a mansion designed by God, a place where tears and fears are wiped away. God gives me the beauty of His creation as a sneak peek into what awaits me. His hand is revealed in every sunrise, each majestic mountain, rushing waterfalls, and hummingbirds.

Although I can't see beyond the waterfall, I am drawn there by God's still voice. He tells me not to focus on the grief and questions of this world but to dream of my forever home. I am reminded to hold on to the things I can't see and trust Jesus' words that are recorded in John 14:2-3: *"My Father's house has many rooms; if that were not so, would I have told you that I am going there to prepare a place for you? And if I go and prepare a place for you, I will come back and take you to be with me that you also may be where I am."*

> *Dear Father, I pray that we may always focus on Your words and trust Your promises. May we run to You when weakness overpowers us and releases our tears and fears. Teach us to foster the fire in our hearts and nurture that spark within us through Your Word and prayer. Remind us to focus on the wonders beyond the waterfalls. Open our eyes and heart to see Your beauty that fills the world, and let us long for our special room that awaits us in our forever home. In Jesus' name I pray. Amen.*

Cookies for God?

Bobbie Bomar Brown

"From the ends of the earth I call to you, I call as my heart grows faint; lead me to the rock that is higher than I. For you have been my refuge, a strong tower against the foe."
-Psalm 61:2-3

I never thought the simple act of recommitting my life to follow Christ would become my refuge. I vowed to give God a hundred percent devotion. But it was God who gave His all to me. His indwelling presence gave hope during the trials that were to come.

The phone woke me, and the nurse quickly explained my daughter had been in a car accident and the doctors were working on her. I pushed for more information, but it was advised I needed to get to the hospital as quickly as possible.

I was met by two police officers who explained the car in which my daughter was a backseat passenger had been rear-ended by a drunk driver. It felt like an eternity before the trauma doctors updated me on her injuries—an open book pelvis break and scalp laceration.

Once she was stabilized, surgery was scheduled for the following morning, but a second X-ray revealed she had a C1 fracture. They immediately placed her in a cervical halo to protect her spinal cord. She was placed in a medicated coma to help with her pain and reduce movement.

They wouldn't allow me to spend another night by her bedside, so I retreated to my motel room. I cried, "Father, please help me be strong, and don't let my daughter die." A peaceful, calming spirit covered me. My crying stopped. I heard, "Don't be afraid. This is what I mean by a hundred percent; give Me all of your fears, anger, and tears. Abide in Me." I fell into a dreamless sleep, woke up the next morning rested, and thanked God for rocking me in His arms.

How foolish I had been, thinking God wanted me to volunteer and bake more cookies; I only needed to surrender and cry for Him.

My daughter had several more setbacks and was hospitalized for over five months. However, I remained strong. I knew God was with me each step.

As I reflect on that time over twenty years ago and of the many heartbreaking phone calls I have since received, I continue to cry and find my refuge in Christ. You can too. He is here for you.

Dear Father, I pray that no matter how many late-night phone calls I receive, I will always cry out to You and feel the warmth of Your hand guiding me through the storms. Create this same peace for others experiencing trials as well. Amen.

Outskirts

Millie Carpenter

"And these are but the outer fringe of his works; how faint the whisper we hear of him! Who then can understand the thunder of his power?"
-Job 26:14

Have you ever looked into someone's eyes as they tried to give you words of encouragement or comfort and wished that you could disappear? Similar to Job's friends confronting him in response to his loss, a cascade of answers, maxims, declarations, and good intentions can crash over us like a wave over a rock—they rush away meaninglessly and void. Worse, they leave behind a rocky spirit that cries out at the injustice of remaining unheard.

Job's friends and our friends try desperately to box up an understanding of God's processes in hopeless situations. In the face of the unknowable and terrifying, pat answers and cliche theological phrases can feel safe, firm, stable. But pat answers cannot save us. And in those moments where we are truly adrift in our grief or pain, that truth is settled deep against our bones. We cannot accept it.

And God invites us not to.

Job's reflection on the vastness of God comforted my heart when no one's words could reach me. Job rejected dogma and responded with an exclamation of the wonder of how little we know of God's being. We know He is beyond us—thunderous! Powerful! But these are just the outskirts of His ways. Just the barest whisper of who God is reaches our ears and our comprehension. Who is God really? We see Him revealed in Jesus. We see Him revealed in the love of others. We see Him in creation, in His Word. We hear testimonies of His love and care. But we have only seen the fringes, the edges of His goodness, of His love, of His power. Maybe that is why He made the universe so vast—so we could see beauty stretching away into infinite space and be staggered by seeing only the margins of the world. So we could know that we have known only the outskirts of Beauty, and of Love, but we will know Him deeper still. Be comforted. This God who we cannot yet fully see or understand has heard us.

Infinite and intimate Savior, thank You that You invite us into naked honesty, true vulnerability, and open hope. Protect us from the well-intentioned words of others. Allow our hearts to rest against You as our firm foundation and greatest love, knowing that we have only begun to know You. Amen.

Pinky Promises

Shelby Perryman

*"Know therefore that the Lord your God is God; he is the faithful
God, keeping his covenant of love to a thousand generations of
those who love him and keep his commandments."*
-Deuteronomy 7:9

Can you remember when you were little and your mom or dad
gave you their pinky finger, telling you to cross yours with theirs? That
was an unbreakable pinky promise. Sometimes they promised fun
things like going out for ice cream after a long day or getting a new toy
because you listened well all week. At other times, it would be an
important child's life event. For example, they would be your biggest
cheerleader at your first soccer game or show up to a school event
where you were nervous. I remember doing this at a very young age
but not understanding what a promise truly meant.

Once my relationship started to grow in Christ, I knew God's
promises were true. Throughout my journey, I haven't always kept my
promises to Christ. I went through quite a few different struggles. A
huge one for me was choosing the wrong men. High school is where I
thought I met my first love. Obviously, we were young and didn't make
the best choices together, but I swore he was the one. I went through a
lot of mental abuse and forgot how to love myself. I did not stand up
for myself or my beliefs. During this relationship, I still believed in
God, but I was going against His truth and knew my relationship

wasn't honoring Him. He asks us to follow biblical principles to show our love for Him so we may have the fullness of life.

After several years, I finally decided enough was enough and ended the relationship. But I kept putting myself in bad situations that were mentally and physically abusive. It was not what I envisioned for my life. I continued to fight and struggle through horrible relationships, knowing deep down in my heart God wanted so much more for me. God is so good and truly did a miracle in my life. Years after all the struggles, He gave me my husband and two beautiful healthy kids. I thank God for them every day.

As an adult, I know the truth of a promise. I understand how much it means both to others and ourselves. Most importantly, I recognize the oath God gave us as Christians. In the above passage, we make a promise to Him, and He makes one to us. He loves us, and in return, we love Him. If we are faithful to Him and follow Him by keeping his commandments, our covenant is unbreakable. That is easier said than done. Without Christ, life can feel impossible. Like a rollercoaster, we constantly go through ups and downs, but as Christians we are called to stand firm in God's promises.

I pray and encourage you to trust in God and His promises no matter what your circumstances. Remember He loves you through everything, and He will forgive you if you truly ask and want forgiveness. I pray you will make the changes in your life that hold you back from having the best relationship of your earthly life with Christ. Please don't ever forget that you are so incredibly loved by Him. If you believe, you will be given eternal life, His ultimate promise and gift. John 3:16 says, "For God so loved the world that he gave his one and only Son, that whoever believes in him shall not perish but have eternal life."

Trusting His Plan

Debra Hill-Gray

"For I know the plans I have for you," declares the Lord, "plans to prosper you and not to harm you, plans to give you hope and a future."
-Jeremiah 29:11

As the labor pains intensified throughout the night, I fought hard to turn my thoughts from the agonizing pain of my broken left humerus, right dislocated shoulder, broken ribs, chest wall abrasions, and all pain from the automobile accident, which just claimed my baby girl's life.

I was seven months gestation, had gone into labor ten days prior, was hospitalized to stop labor, discharged to home, and on my way back to my follow-up with my OB-GYN when we had the head-on collision. My doctors had no way of knowing this tragedy would happen. They'd delivered my first stillborn daughter less than a year before and were trying to prevent another loss.

I was 23, and just weeks before had publicly professed the gift of salvation from Jesus and was baptized with my husband.

As I fought to turn my thoughts from pain to something else, I felt the only thing to look forward to was holding her in my arms once delivered. I'd study her angelic face, kiss her tiny feet, unwrap her from her blanket to soak in every inch of her—to feel like I had a baby for an hour. I'd called her "Angel Baby" throughout my entire pregnancy, for reasons I didn't know. But she was just that—the perfect image of an angel! When it was time, I handed her to the nurse to take my Amanda away.

I turned my focus to God. I prayed. I told Him I knew He had a reason for needing her with Him. I knew He had His plan. I never asked Him why. I began the grieving process, knowing it wasn't in His plans yet for me to have a baby. The emotional and physical abuse that followed from her father may have been why, but I didn't need to know.

I had a solid trust and foundation in Christ and a new, strong relationship with Him, which were enough. These sustained me. This is not to say it was always like this throughout my life. But it was then.

Our trust in God develops from building a strong relationship with Him, learning Scripture, and through our prayers and conversations with Him. We must keep our relationship with God on a solid foundation, knowing He will always meet our needs, even in times of deep sorrow.

God blessed me with a beautiful baby boy less than two years later, and two beautiful girls, after a miscarriage before I had them, but I always trusted He would.

Father, show us how to build a stronger foundation with You each new day. Help us put all of our trust in You, knowing You have plans to give us hope and a future, not in our time, but in Yours. Thank You for the comfort You provide during our times of sorrow. Amen.

Unbreakable Promise

Bobbie Bomar Brown

"Be strong and courageous. Do not be afraid or terrified because of them, for the Lord your God goes with you; he will never leave you nor forsake you."
-Deuteronomy 31:6

The silence of my mountain home was disrupted. The neighbors' horse neighed and paced the corral. Her deep cries shook the window I watched from. I feared a mountain lion or bear threatened her or her colt. I rushed outside. The only intruder I spotted was a horse trailer vanishing down the street.

The beautiful mare ran to the edge of the fence as if to jump over but lowered her head and jerked back, releasing a cry that pierced my heart. I sat helpless for hours, watching and hoping for the return of her young; I wanted the pain this mother felt to stop. I am not sure why the mare finally stopped searching and quietness filled the air. Did she give up hope and accept a piece of her was gone forever?

I have moved into a new season of life; my heart cries for the emptiness I feel as I struggle to accept the reality that a part of me is missing and I will never see my son again. However, God whispered His truth and replaced my pain with renewed hope that I will join my son once again in our forever home. I now envision my son sitting with Jesus, sharing his poetry, and he is pain free.

My cries have slowed down, and the search for my son has lessened. I found the only weapon against this pain is the comfort I find in Jesus' words that He speaks to me daily through the Holy Bible, friends, and devotions. When sickness or death invades our world, I know the deep cries of the heart often drown out God's whispers, but we must remain strong and believe in His unbreakable promise: Deuteronomy 31:8: *"The Lord himself goes before you and will be with you; he will never leave you nor forsake you. Do not be afraid; do not be discouraged."*

Oh Father, it is Your strength that provides the brokenhearted peace and calms our cries. I pray when life is hard, we run to You, cling to Your promises, and let You calm the panic within us. "Blessed is the one who perseveres under trial because, having stood the test, that person will receive the crown of life that the Lord has promised to those who love him" (James 1:12).

Waiting

Jordan Ramos

"Many are the plans in a person's heart, but it is the Lord's purpose that prevails."
-Proverbs 19:21

God starts and ends every day with the perfect gift of a sunrise and sunset. Shades of pink, yellow, and orange melding together remind us of His beauty in creation.

I was on the phone with my grandmother, and she gave me a fresh perspective on the sunrise. She said she loves the way the sunrise takes its time each morning. Rather than startling us with a bright light, the light is gradual. The timing of the sun rising in the sky is perfect. God's timing is perfect. Proverbs 19:21 reminds us that although we like to make plans, it is God's purpose that prevails.

We may feel God is silent during the waiting, or we even feel forgotten. We may be waiting on a devotion to take flight, on a child to come back to Christ, or for a diagnosis, the right job, a husband or wife to change their ways, or answers to repeated prayers. Waiting is hard, especially because Satan loves to tear us down with lies. The enemy doesn't want us to wait on God's provision because he knows God's plan will be better for us than what we can plan on our own. Satan shouts while God whispers. What lies are you believing?

God's timing is perfect because He strengthens us in the waiting. Oftentimes we want things done quickly, but then we miss out on the growth God has for us on the journey. All we need to do is trust that the Lord Almighty has power over our life and be still.

"The Lord is my shepherd, I lack nothing. He makes me lie down in green pastures, he leads me beside quiet waters, he refreshes my soul. He guides me along the right paths for his name's sake. Even though I walk through the darkest valley, I will fear no evil, for you are with me; your rod and your staff, they comfort me. You prepare a table before me in the presence of my enemies. You anoint my head with oil; my cup overflows. Surely your goodness and love will follow me all the days of my life, and I will dwell in the house of the Lord forever" (Psalm 23:1-6).

Dear Lord,
Thank you for the reminder that your plans are always better
than mine. Lord, strengthen me in the waiting. Grow our
relationship in the waiting. I trust You with _____.
I know You have me and love me, and I am confident knowing
You have a purpose for me.
In Jesus' name I pray. Amen.

When There's Nowhere to Go

Millie Carpenter

"Simon Peter answered him, 'Lord, to whom shall we go? You have the words of eternal life. We have come to believe and to know that you are the Holy One of God.'"
-John 6:68-69

Peter and the disciples faced the choice to continue following Jesus in His daily ministry after hearing Him say difficult things they could not understand. Jeremiah 14 has parallel prayers to God, exclaiming dependence on God amid pain and disaster with a cry of "Do not leave us" (Jeremiah 14:9 ESV).

During a year of devastating circumstances, the loss of family members, hurt, betrayal, fear, and uncertainty, I look at these words and think of distinct moments. I see myself in a car with my head against the steering wheel, mouth open in a wordless cry to God for understanding and comfort. I see myself awake in the dark of night, tossing and turning, the sharp words of others in my mind, wondering how to respond without bitterness—or wondering if I even wanted to try. I see myself sitting on top of a mountain I climbed my whole life and revisited, almost like a pilgrimage, in response to my pain: tears staining my cheeks as the cold wind kissed them away.

There's a clarity to these moments of my life, not only because of the pain in them, but because they were crossroads. Consciously or unconsciously, I faced a choice in each of these moments: to hold my brokenness open to God despite my lack of understanding—or to walk away. There's no formula for being met by God in these crossroads, and each person will have different moments, but the choice is the same. Does Jesus have the words of eternal life? Do we believe, even if we do not understand Him, that He loves us and is willing to hear our pain?

Sometimes we make the choice to continue the path of believing simply because there is nowhere else to go. Jesus still accepts us. He knows us. While in these moments we may believe there is nothing more happening to us than life-bleeding hurt, Jesus steps in to redeem and bring new life. I look back on my moments and still feel the pain. But I also feel Christ's overwhelming love. I see the path He led me down. I see when I stayed simply because I had nowhere else to go, He still comforted me. And the place He led me is good. He is good.

Oh Giver of Eternal Life, at times our souls are crushed, tired, hungry, and even angry. We wonder about the surrounding devastation. But You are eternal. You yourself are Life. Be Life to us in our moments most marked by death. Be our Peace in uncertainty. Help us to choose You at our crossroads of helplessness. Encourage us, Lord, when we cling to You only because there is nowhere else to go. And bring us each day more into Your life and glory. Amen.

Trust in God

Place your full trust
in His unfailing love
and provision

Enduring the Race

Niki Barlow

"…let us throw off everything that hinders and the sin that so easily entangles. And let us run with perseverance the race marked out for us, fixing our eyes on Jesus, the pioneer and perfecter of faith…."
-Hebrews 12:1-2

The velvety darkness was broken with the sprinkle of glittery stars. A light streaked across the sky, then was gone. For one glorious moment, the meteor's usual dark matter turned bright and shiny, erupting into an amazing flash, but it burned up, leaving nothing.

We can be like that too. I watched a whirlwind of human energy run through the room, grabbing anything left out. The washer was going, counters wiped down, and toys removed, leaving clean surfaces. Things were now hidden from view, but under the counters and behind the doors was a chaotic mess. After a few days of this, the woman was exhausted. Her energy was gone, buried under tears.

Sometimes we pull up our adrenaline and run with an idea, project, or circumstance, shoving all our energy, time, and resources into it, only to be defeated in the end by our own inability to sustain such high energy. When the crash comes, we curl up, eat comfort food, or isolate ourselves.

God never intended for us to have these cycles. He loves us and fills us with His holy presence, providing us with life-giving energy, which overflows to those around us. He does not expect or want us to give all of ourselves away, leaving nothing but pain, hurt, or tiredness.

If we go before Him, we take it upon ourselves to make things happen. When our efforts do not produce the effect we want, we wonder why things are not working. Take the time to ask God to lead and align your thoughts and desires with His. You can do this through prayer and Scripture.

Recognize when you are striving in your own strength. Instead, slow down and take a breath. When you are weary, take a break. Read a book, sit outside with a cup of tea, talk to your family or friends, watch the sunset, and know you are not alone. Fix your eyes forward on Jesus. He is perfecting you. He will bring fulfillment, peace, and contentment, allowing the restlessness of your soul to dissipate.

Father, help us let go of our activities, our plans, and the sins of this world so that we will run the race You have set before us well. Perfect us, growing endurance and wisdom within us. May we always feel Your presence and be firm in the knowledge You never leave us. We recognize we can mess up our lives easily, but when we follow Your plans, we find joy, love, and fulfillment. Where we have wavered, bring us back to your path predestined for us. Let us be content to be where You want us to be. Amen.

The Flood

Trudy Hewitt

"Who shall separate us from the love of Christ? Shall trouble or hardship or persecution or famine or nakedness or danger or sword?"

-Romans 8:35

The day was July 27, 1997. I was a leader on the Colorado State University campus in Fort Collins, Colorado, helping to set up for a large youth conference. Three thousand high schoolers were arriving soon with more staff from all over the United States, and we were getting ready for them as rain began to fall that evening.

We leaders watched in dismay as three inches of rain fell every hour. Floodwater rose and inundated the campus. The next day, it became apparent that we were in the midst of a major flood. As we met that morning for a cold breakfast, prayed, and tried to decide what to do, workers arrived and began to haul furniture out of buildings. We discussed canceling the conference, but it seemed impossible to do so at that late date.

Our computers were knocked out. We didn't know where three thousand kids were supposed to sleep or even meet, but God did. He helped us begin the momentous job of rebuilding a conference that had taken us months to build—without those computers. The chorus of the song "God Leads Us Along" begins, "Some through the waters, some through the flood," which became our theme song.

Often in times of trouble, people turn to God in much greater numbers. This seemed especially true of teens. Our staff, so accustomed to working with teens and observing this trait, had also learned this. We worked for 48 hours straight, assigning students to dorms, to meeting rooms, to mealtimes.

Kids and their leaders arrived and waited while things were set up and the conference began. As kids walked to different buildings for meetings, weaving among piles and piles of wet furniture from the dorms and classrooms, the Spirit of God pulled them closer to Him and closer to each other. The conference was a mess but a huge success!

As we face troubled times, we need to always remember that God is in control. We can trust Him, He loves us, and ***nothing*** can separate us from Him.

Father, sometimes the lessons You teach us are quite painful. As I have learned through each one, I see myself growing in faith and learning to trust You. Each time I see that, a warmth grows inside me, and each time my faith grows, my ability to survive hardship grows as well. Thank You for the life lessons as I learn to trust You more and more each time. Amen.

Spiritual Drift

Greg Grandchamp

*"...I pray that you, being rooted and established in love, may
have power, together with all the Lord's holy people, to grasp how
wide and long and high and deep is the love of Christ, and to
know this love that surpasses knowledge—that you may be filled
to the measure of all the fullness of God."*
-Ephesians 3:17-19

You wake up one day and realize that you have been drifting
away from the Lord. Oh, you still believe—but somehow your faith,
your commitment, is not quite where it had been. You haven't picked
up your Bible in quite a while, and you rarely pray anymore. Life just
seems to have gotten in the way, and you let it. And when you do pray,
your prayers seem shallow and procedural. Empty. You're not even
sure anymore if God is listening.

Spiritual drift. You know what it is because you can feel it. Life
can most certainly be hard. Sometimes it feels like there is no end in
sight to the challenges—or even pain and grief. Maybe we then let
ourselves kind of drift from the light into the gray area—getting way
too close to the darkness.

How in the world did you let yourself fall so far, so fast? But it
happened, and when you think about it, you hate it. But ask yourself:
How do I get that back?

There are times in everyone's life when we have felt hopeless. When we have felt joyless. Or when we felt like there was chaos all around us. But what can bring us back to a foundation of complete joy and peace—and trust — is the message brought to us by Christ Jesus. The message of eternal hope and trust in Him. The message that caused you to give your life to Him to begin with.

When we gave our lives to Jesus, it meant a change in us. Remember, the same Spirit that raised Christ from the dead resides in us. In you (Romans 8:11). That means that the same power that raised our Savior from the dead lives within you and can bring you not just the hope of eternity, but also the peace, the joy, and the trust that can shape and embolden our lives here on earth.

He's waiting for your return with open arms.

Father, help me return to You. Help me go back to my first love. I need You now more than I think I ever have, and yet I know I have drifted. Please help me go back to my first love. I need to trust You again, to feel Your loving embrace. Please help me, Father. Amen.

The Lord Shepherds Me

Katie Erickson

"The Lord is my shepherd, I lack nothing. He makes me lie down in green pastures, he leads me beside quiet waters."
-Psalm 23:1-2

Psalm 23 is likely the most well-known psalm, or perhaps even one of the most well-known passages in the Bible. It's often used at funerals or other times when people are seeking comfort and peace in the midst of life's difficulties.

Psalm 23:1 says, *"The Lord is my shepherd, I lack nothing."* A more direct translation from Hebrew would be: "The Lord shepherds me, I will not lack."

The word for shepherd is what's called a participle, which implies continuous action. It's kind of a cross between a verb (an action word) and a noun (a thing), and it has the word for "me" attached to it. So, the idea is the Lord is continually shepherding me through all things.

Sheep have many needs that the shepherd must care for. Sheep do not "just take care of themselves," as some might suppose. More than any other class of livestock, they require endless attention and meticulous care. We humans are pretty needy too, and God promises here in this verse that when we are truly following Him, He will meet all our needs, and we won't lack anything.

Psalm 23:2 says, "He makes me lie down in green pastures, he leads me beside quiet waters."

A more direct Hebrew translation says, "In dwelling places of grass, He causes me to lie down. Beside waters of rest, He intently leads me."

The key thing to note here is the intentionality of the verbs. He *causes* me to lie down; it's not like, "Oh, while you're here, maybe lie down if you want." We often don't want to rest and stop our productivity, but we need the Lord to make us stop! It is only through God that we truly can lie down and find rest, regardless of whether we are in a time of hurt or a time of joy in our lives.

God does not just lead us beside quiet waters, but He does so intensely and intentionally. The connotation of that Hebrew verb is one of intentionality, of being led with purpose. It is not just an aimless wandering, but rather a specific, intentional direction in which He leads us. It is God's purpose that we are near these quiet waters, regardless of where the world is trying to lead us. The Lord is being very intentional about leading us. He is leading us on purpose and with a plan.

Place your trust in God, who shepherds His people, causes us to rest in Him, and intentionally leads us where He wants us to go.

The Lord Restores and Protects Me

Katie Erickson

"…he refreshes my soul. He guides me along the right paths for his name's sake."
-Psalm 23:3

A more literal Hebrew translation of Psalm 23:3 would be: "My soul He restores. He causes to conduct me in paths of righteousness for the sake of His name."

The verb for "restores" has the idea of bringing something back. This intensive verb implies intentionality. The Lord is intent on taking care of us, His people, intentionally and with purpose. When we stray from Him, the Lord always wants to bring us back and restore us! This is a full restoration of our souls that can only happen through Jesus.

The verb for "guides" is a causative form, showing that the Lord is guiding us and nudging us to do something. Here, He is guiding us to walk in the paths of righteousness. God knows that in our own strength, we'll wander off His righteous paths and go toward the ways of the world.

Psalm 23:4 reads, "Even though I walk through the darkest valley, I will fear no evil, for you are with me; your rod and your staff, they comfort me."

This valley is a place of utter darkness and gloom. Some older translations called it "the valley of the shadow of death," but the Hebrew word is closer to darkness or gloom than death.

At times, we may feel that we are in a place of utter darkness. But we fear no evil because *You*, God, are with us, even in this place of deep despair! The word "you" is written out in Hebrew, which shows that this is for emphasis. God, our shepherd, is with us.

It is because of the shepherd's actions in verse 3 of restoring us and leading us in righteousness that this lack of fear in verse 4 is possible. While we may wonder why the shepherd doesn't just lead the sheep around this valley of darkness rather than through it, that's generally not how God works. We grow in our faith and mature as Christians when we go through trials, as this valley alludes to.

The last phrase of the verse describes the tools of the shepherd—the rod and the staff. The rod conveys the concept of authority, discipline, and defense against danger. The staff speaks of all that is long-suffering and kind. These tools represent God constantly watching over His own and bringing comfort because of His presence and involvement with His sheep.

We trust in God because He is the one who restores our souls,
and He leads and guides us even in the darkest times.

The Lord Pursues Me

Katie Erickson

"You prepare a table before me in the presence of my enemies.
You anoint my head with oil; my cup overflows."
-Psalm 23:5

If the words of Psalm 23:4 are true, that we fear no evil because God is with us, then we are able to even eat with those whom we fear might attack us! That's the power of the almighty God at work in our lives; that's why we can trust Him.

The phrase "you anoint my head with oil" could literally be translated as "you make my head fat with fat." The ideas of anointing, oil, and fat refer to richness. In that culture, if you were fat, then you must be rich because you clearly had plenty to eat and didn't have to expend much effort for it, as opposed to those people who had to work hard labor for each meal.

We have that through God—He did all the work for us through Jesus on the cross. All we need to do is to have faith in Him, and He will make us rich in His grace, so much so that our cup overflows! This is another image of not only having enough but having plenty. The Hebrew for this phrase literally says, "my cup is saturated."

The imagery of the overflowing cup looks back to the "I will not lack" phrase from Psalm 23:1. The cup symbolizes the care and provision of God, and it can also be linked to the banquet imagery of the table. The cup the host offers to his guest is filled to the brim with wine as a gesture of generosity. God generously gives to us when we follow Him as a sheep follows its shepherd.

Psalm 23:6 says, "Surely your goodness and love will follow me all the days of my life, and I will dwell in the house of the Lord forever."

The Hebrew word for "goodness" here refers to the total perfection of God's original creation (Genesis 1:31). The word for love here is the Hebrew concept of *hesed*—a combination of love, mercy, compassion, and kindness. These attributes will not just "follow" us, but the Hebrew word means to chase or pursue us. Perfection and *hesed* are not only following us but are literally chasing after us.

We will dwell with the Lord for the length of our days. Even when we have trouble on this earth, when we trust in God, we know we will have a joyous homecoming of being in the Lord's house for the rest of our days.

The Possibilities of the "What-Ifs"

Kirsten Wegele

"Ask and it will be given to you; seek and you will find; knock and the door will be opened to you. For everyone who asks receives; the one who seeks finds; and to the one who knocks, the door will be opened."
-Matthew 7:7-8

Imagine sitting in the possibilities of the "what-ifs," the "what-ifs" of our future. The "what-if" of what I have been praying and hoping for actually coming true. The "what-ifs" that allow us to dream and run again. The "what-ifs" that propel us into the greater calling, the destiny that He wants to fulfill in us.

It's in the moments of the "what-ifs" that our faith is **stretched** and increases because we're thinking in a new heavenly perspective. It is one where there's no doubt or fear, but rather the gap between the impossible is bridged and met by the possible. It's the "what-ifs" of God that will sustain us in living out "His Kingdom come."

I once heard "think higher" than what you are feeling and experiencing. There is so much truth and freedom in that. We are called to think in a heavenly perspective and not off of our own emotions. Our emotions are ever-changing, but one thing that ***always*** remains is His ways, His mindset. Sometimes God will speak words we may think are "ridiculous," but they may be the most important words to hold on to. They are the "what-if" words of what God *can* do. It's that building of "risk-taking" in your faith that will exceed where you've been and where He has you.

I encourage you to remember that the staple of your "being" is Jesus! Look past and ***beyond*** what your eyes can see of the future to what His future holds for you. Look past your own insecurities and your own emotions and ***extend*** your faith to see the goodness of God working. Declare the things that He has for you and ***stand*** on the words that He has spoken to you.

"Very truly I tell you, whoever believes in me will do the works I have been doing, and they will do even greater things than these, because I am going to the Father. And I will do whatever you ask in my name, so that the Father may be glorified in the Son. You may ask me for anything in my name, and I will do it" (John 14:12-14).

Declare this: Lord, You know everything about me. You perceive every movement of my heart and soul, and You understand my every thought before it ever enters my mind. You are so intimately aware of me, Lord. You read my heart like an open book, and You know all the words I'm about to speak before I even start a sentence! You know every step that I will take before my journey begins. You've gone into my future to prepare the way, and in kindness You follow behind me to spare me from the harm of my past. You hold every moment, and everything You do is marvelously breathtaking. I am thankful that You are always thinking of me!

Worry or Trust? Our Choice

Greg Grandchamp

"Who of you by worrying can add a single hour to your life? Since you cannot do this very little thing, why do you worry about the rest?"
-Luke 12:25-26

What is truly accomplished by worry? Nothing. Yet, trusting in God—really, truly trusting—is not always easy. In fact, it is often very hard to truly trust God. We so often say we give it to Him and then take it right back as if He isn't capable. Too often, the challenge is that our prayer is for the outcome we want—rather than for God's will to be done, with confidence that He knows what is best for us. And maybe therein lies the answer.

Sometimes we are like children asking their parents for something they want, but the parents know all too well that in the long run, what their children are asking for is not best or even good for them. Like any good Father, the Lord always knows what is best for us, even when we do not.

We cannot help but be astonished by the strength and faith displayed by Shadrach, Meshach, and Abednego in Daniel 3. By their faith in God—the one true God. By their confidence that God is who

He says He is and will do what He says He will do. By their utmost faith in the supreme being who they knew had the power to deliver them, one way or another. The only one who could.

But how do we get there? How do we overcome the anxiety that is hammering our hearts? Well, the closer we get to God, the easier it becomes. When we give it to Him, really give it to Him, and pray that His will be done—well, suddenly we know that whatever happens, it will be for the best.

What is troubling you today? Is your heart burdened because of some problem that threatens to overcome you? Are you filled with anxiety and worry, wondering what will happen next? Listen—as a child of God through faith in Christ, you can turn these over to Christ, knowing that He loves you and is able to help you. Don't carry your burden any longer. Bring it "boldly to the throne of grace"—and leave it there.

Father, it would be a lie to say I'm not worried. But I am turning to you, Lord. Help me to overcome my worries and my anxiety. Help me to overcome those worries with complete trust in You, Father. Help me to know, really know. I give it all to You, Lord. Amen.

Fostering the Heart

Embrace healing and growth, as He gently mends wounded hearts

A Smoldering Coal

Niki Barlow

*"But the fruit of the Spirit is love, joy, peace, forbearance,
kindness, goodness, faithfulness, gentleness and self-control.
Against such things there is no law. Those who belong to Christ
Jesus have crucified the flesh with its passions and desires. Since
we live by the Spirit, let us keep in step with the Spirit."*
-Galatians 5:22-25

The night was cool, but the campfire kept us warm. The flames flickered in a rhythmic dance. Sipping on tea, I watched my two-year-old covered in dirt joyfully playing with rocks. As the flames died down, we got ready to slip into our sleeping bags. I poured water over the remaining coals, extinguishing the fire.

Late at night, the wind whipped through the trees, rocking our brightly lit tent. I knew that was not right. I pulled back the entrance cover to see a frenzy of raging flames flicking up five feet into the sky. It took only one small coal to spark into an inferno. Fortunately, I got it out.

A single smoldering coal within a person can lead to unrest. Have you ever had a moment where you were angry at someone for something they said, but instead of confronting them, you let it fester until it erupted in a string of emotion and words you did not mean? It causes hurt, pain, and roadblocks to your relationship.

Opposite to smoldering is the inferno when you react instantly and regret your words almost immediately. Your reaction was not important, or you misunderstood the other person. In society, we are surrounded by misunderstandings, communication issues, and hatred built on misconceptions.

The good news is that God's redemption is ours because He is forgiving and loving. He is our example. Instead of being a spark which causes discontent, Christians are called to show kindness, goodness, faithfulness, gentleness, and self-control. All these actions are achievable while being led by the Holy Spirit.

Being a flame provides the light of Jesus and shows a pathway to new life. A flicker is gentle, easing others toward God instead of pushing them away. Our kind words lift and encourage people to become their best selves. We have opportunities to say life-giving or death-causing words. Choose to bring joy instead of anger. You and the person you are talking to will have a better day and a chance of deeper conversation drawing you closer together.

Father, thank You for Your redeeming love. Even when we make mistakes, You allow us to ask for forgiveness. We pray today our words will reflect Yours. Let our conversations be sweet and uplifting. Give us the self-control necessary to stop hurtful words. Let us be a part of bringing joy to others. Amen.

Be Transformed

Millie Carpenter

"And we all, who with unveiled faces contemplate the Lord's glory, are being transformed into his image with ever-increasing glory, which comes from the Lord, who is the Spirit."
- 2 Corinthians 3:18

God's people are an integral way that He communicates to us His glory, His love, His comfort. This truth approached me slowly, flitting over several years to settle against my spirit, but holding me up like a foundation stone when I needed it most.

The reality of this drifted to me through the mentorship of older women in my church throughout my youth, who encouraged my gifts, but who changed me the most by the way their way of living called me to account. Seeing the way they welcomed people into their homes, sacrificed their time, or chose to support others shifted the way I saw myself and the world around me. I experienced being loved through intense emotions over a steaming cup of tea, experienced being prayed for verbally, experienced the invitation to sit before a warm fire and simply exist—and I was transformed. Who and how I wanted to be in the world changed through interacting in the real world with people who chose to embody God's empathy, care, and sacrificial love.

Relationships transform us. As we see others for who they truly are and experience the freedom of being ourselves, the exchange itself remakes us. Each person we meet is a small unveiling of God's own presence in the world. A small invitation to transformation. A small reminder that while we are with others, we cannot claim that God has not heard us, that God is not with us, that God will not speak to us—because He does all this through His everyday servants. Through tea before bed, warm tortilla soup, walks on dirt roads, and reminders to rest from the people who surround us. What a relief! We do not have to ascend to heaven to encounter the divine. He chooses to speak through our neighbors, especially when we have to lean close to hear His voice there.

Thank You, Father, that You are transforming us into Your loving, glorious image. Forgive us for overlooking Your image in the face of our neighbor so often. Open our eyes to the words of life and comfort and to the listening ear that You extend to us through Your people. Remake us to be like You as we see You more clearly—unveiled each day a little more as we behold You in worship, in fellowship, and in communion. Amen.

Forgiveness

Greg Grandchamp

"Bear with each other and forgive one another if any of you has a grievance against someone. Forgive as the Lord forgave you."
-Colossians 3:13

You have been hurt deeply. By someone you loved and trusted, no less. And it was painful. Deeply painful. We have all experienced it at some point in our lives. Whether it was your parents, someone else in your family, a close friend, or someone at work, you're feeling it and just can't get over it. They have apologized—but you can't find it in you to forgive them.

The question we must each ask ourselves is: Why? What is preventing us from forgiving someone who has offended us? Maybe we think they don't really deserve it. Maybe we want to get them back and let them experience what it feels like. Then—and only then—you'll forgive. But then we must also ask ourselves: What makes us think we deserve the forgiveness of God?

Perhaps the most amazing part of the good news of Jesus Christ is that He died for us while we were still sinners. While we were still His enemy, He suffered and gave His life so we could be forgiven. That's simply overwhelming when we let ourselves think about it. And it makes our forgiveness of others just a bit easier. God has offered us the mercy of forgiveness—and we are called to be merciful in the same way to others.

We must remember that forgiveness of others releases us from the bondage of anger and resentment. It releases the grudge we carry around with us that steals our peace and our joy. Our forgiveness may be meaningless to the ones who have hurt us. They may go on with their lives without a hint of remorse or guilt over what they have done. Their happiness remains while yours is tied up in knots. When we see them, we get a little twist in our gut—even, maybe especially, if we have never said anything to them about how they hurt us.

Often, we don't know how to get there. Well, God knows that, and His Spirit will help us if we're honest with Him. If we seek His help. A good place to start is by simply uttering the words "I forgive," then praying that the Lord will help you feel it and believe it.

Glorious Father, thank You. Thank You for Your forgiveness, for Your mercy and grace. Thank You for sending Your Son to bear my sins. Please help me, Father. Help me to find it in my heart to forgive as You have forgiven me when I didn't deserve it. Amen.

Love with Legs

Joe Pierce

"And now these three remain: faith, hope and love. But the greatest of these is love"
-1 Corinthians 13:13

The word "love" is an overused word. We love the new drink at our favorite coffee shop or the shirt in the window of our favorite mall store. A teen couple says, "Love you," as they part ways at her English class, and the teacher who overhears chuckles and thinks to herself, *Someday you will understand love, and chances are it won't be with the baseball player who just walked you to class.*

The love I speak of is the love God has for us and calls us to exhibit in our lives. It is love that He wants to pour out on others through us.

"Greater love has no one than this: to lay down one's life for one's friends" (John 15:13).

This love is selfless, sacrificial, unconditional, enduring, and forgiving.

It's loving those who have wronged us and those others see as unlovable. It is loving strangers as we love family. Sometimes, all we can do is love and pray from afar.

"Whoever does not love does not know God, because God is love" (1 John 4:8).

The word "love" appears close to four hundred times in the Bible. It was at the core of what Jesus taught and calls us into. In Matthew 22:36-39, Jesus, when asked what the greatest commandment is, answered, "'Love the Lord your God with all your heart and with all your soul and with all your mind.' This is the first and greatest commandment. And the second is like it: 'Love your neighbor as yourself.'" Simple, right? Nope! Because we are human and destined to fail. Because we are easily hurt or offended. It is even more difficult to love someone who has caused us genuine pain and hardship.

Unconditional love and forgiveness are very hard.

Reverend Billy Graham once said: "Only God can give us a selfless love for others as the Holy Spirit changes us from within. This is one reason we must receive Christ, for apart from His Spirit we can never be freed from the chains of selfishness, jealousy, and indifference. Will others see Christ's love in your life today?"

So, my question for you?

Does your love have legs?

Do you walk it out? Are you striving to walk in the love God calls us to share?

We will never truly walk out the love that God calls us to, that Jesus displayed.

But we can look for ways each day to love others, show kindness to strangers, show grace, and forgive freely. We can ensure that our love has legs.

Playing Frisbee

Trudy Hewitt

*"...so that you do not grieve like the rest of mankind, who have
no hope."*
-1 Thessalonians 4:13

My mom moved to a nursing home in our town in 2015. My
baby sister was put on hospice across the hall, where she died of colon
cancer three days later. It was a gift for my mom to be there in Cheri's
final days.

Three weeks later, Mom was diagnosed with zero potassium.
The doctor said one cannot live without potassium. Nothing they did
could get her levels up.

We were traveling in the ministry at the time, and the doctor
would call us to come. We would rush home and ***always***, Mom would
be sitting up in bed. "Hi," she'd say, smiling broadly.

This went on for five months, ***without potassium in her body***.

Finally, as we left for a ministry convention one Thursday, I
told Mom that Cheri was in heaven, waiting for her, and that we'd be
OK if she went to heaven, too. "OK?" I said. "OK!" she nodded,
smiling radiantly.

The next morning, as my hand reached for the hotel door
handle, my phone rang. I knew. The nurse said Mom had passed that
morning. She asked when I was coming. I said, "Monday."

"You're not coming?"

"I know where she is."

"You're not coming?"

"That's just a shell. You have everything you need in your computer."

"You're not coming?" (three times)

"I'm here with two hundred of my closest friends. I am where I need to be. I will see you on Monday."

I called my husband, who was downstairs, and I told him that Mom was gone. I said, "I can tell you, but I cannot say it again." He understood, and he told people for me.

At the convention, people hugged me, cried, and prayed all day. It was wonderful, and it was horrible.

The next morning, I headed down early to the leadership breakfast to help, as I always did. A woman approached me, her arms held out. I knew I couldn't do a repeat of the day before—and then a light dawned for me! Three teens had died in our town that year. When we told the youth group kids, they hugged, cried, and prayed, then went out to play Frisbee.

I said to the woman, "Do you know what teenagers do when a friend dies? They hug, pray and cry, then go play Frisbee. Today, I need to play Frisbee." People understood, and it was a wonderful day.

I learned that when grief overwhelms, we sometimes just need to play Frisbee.

Father, You are Love. Thank You for the hope You've given us.

This Little Light of Mine

Debra Hill-Gray

"You are the light of the world. A town built on a hill cannot be hidden. Neither do people light a lamp and put it under a bowl. Instead they put it on its stand, and it gives light to everyone in the house. In the same way, let your light shine before others, that they may see your good deeds and glorify your Father in heaven"
-Matthew 5:14-16

As our world becomes progressively more accepting of sinful nature, I ponder: How can I be a better witness amid the chaos? How do I instill a strong foundation of Christianity in my grandchildren and their generation? How will I help those with no exposure to Christianity understand and accept the gift of salvation?

In my work and volunteer efforts with individuals who struggle with addiction, I've heard a stupendous amount of "no's" when asked, "Do you believe in God?" My response is always, "It is God who leads me to help you." Diving deeper into their stories, most were diagnosed with post-traumatic stress disorder from "adverse childhood experiences" (ACE). Many come from dysfunctional homes. The cycle continued into adulthood. They had no exposure to the Bible. Most adult children of dysfunctional families don't realize their lives were abnormal. Having been through things no child should ever experience, they're accustomed to a life of chaos. No one told them how Jesus could make their lives better.

Some answered "yes," usually those in recovery. That's the miracle of salvation. There's a renewed hope that comes with living our rebirth in Christ, finding purpose in transparency, and becoming wonderful witnesses to others. Testimonies bring others from darkness into the light!

Moreover, social media has become an unyielding platform for casting sinful behaviors to screens, easily accessible to anyone with a device and Wi-Fi. Children and teens are exposed to the world's way, being sculpted with that foundation instead of the loving foundation of God. Unless adults monitor their children's screens and teach them about God, they understand life as shown on social media to be the norm. As Christians, we know it is not.

Where do I fit in with my ability to witness to others? I ask myself this all the time. I've concluded that witnessing is not my strong suit. I tend to push my beliefs too firmly, which pushes people further from my very purpose.

I've finally accepted that my witnessing comes in the form of the light others see in me. I don't have to try explaining the Gospel to every nonbeliever—that isn't my gift. I just need to keep living my life as an obedient Christian. While I'm far from perfect and have walked my own dark roads, I remain cognizant that everyone I encounter is watching. People hear the words I speak and the tone I use. They take note of my kindness, as well as my weaknesses. I must purposefully live fully in God's presence and by His commandments for others to understand the light shining through me comes from my life being lived for Him.

I don't need to preach or teach. I merely need to be myself, letting God's light shine brightly through me!

Heavenly Father, please help Your light shine brightly through us as we live as obedient Christians. Help those walking in darkness to see the light radiating through us as a lamp to guide them toward hope and a renewed life in the gift of salvation.

Those on Whom His Favor Rests

Karren Mitchell

"Glory to God in the highest heaven, and on earth peace to those on whom his favor rests."
-Luke 2:14

Every Christmas, we hear: "peace on earth, goodwill toward men." We see that phrase on Christmas cards and chant it in the lovely, nostalgic Christmas carols we share. But what does it mean? The NIV Bible translates it as someone "on whom His favor rests." The KJV translation says, "good will toward men."

I have often wondered about the meaning of this passage. Moreover, how can I be a person of goodwill or one on whom God's favor rests?

Following the Ten Commandments from the Law of Moses is a start. Jesus, however, brought still another requirement, perhaps the hardest requirement. He commands us to love one another.

In this age of such divisiveness, it is easy to think that we only have to love those who think like us or look like us. It is still easier to think our neighbors are only the ones who live next door to us.

Every major religion on this planet has some form of the Golden Rule, which entreats us to behave toward others as we would want them to behave toward us. All of that is just another way of saying: Love one another. Why is it so difficult to get past the differences in our personalities, customs, languages, and ways of worshipping? Can we call ourselves the favored of God or people of goodwill if we harbor hatred for even one of our brothers or sisters?

If, when we look at another person, all we see is the difference in skin color, dress, accent, or religion, then we are missing the humanity of that person and the things we have in common.

There is so much suffering in this world that it is easy to give up on trying. What can I do that makes a difference? Does that exempt us from even trying?

We can start each day striving to change ourselves and the way we look at others. We can do one thing that is kind for someone that looks different from ourselves. Will it make a difference? Yes! It will make a difference in the life of the person to whom we show kindness, and it will make a difference in us. How can we be one of the favored of God? By being one who loves His children—all of His children.

Wiped Clean

Joe Pierce

"...for all have sinned and fall short of the glory of God, and all are justified freely by his grace through the redemption that came by Christ Jesus"
-Romans 3:23-24

My early life, especially in middle and high school, was saturated with violence.

That violence manifested itself in many ways. Schools still paddled kids back then, and parents still spanked. My dad definitely walked just this side of "too far." He had a belt, and when he really got carried away, you would catch the buckle sometimes in the frenzy.

Outside the home, a lot of my time was spent fighting. Often, I would "defend" someone I saw as weak or bullied in some way. That was my rationalization for times when rage should have been restraint.

By the grace of God, my father's propensity to physical violence at home never manifested itself in my relationship with my late wife. Thankfully, that generational curse ended with me. But coming home a little worse for wear still happened occasionally, and we were often verbally abusive to one another.

Some years later, we found ourselves back in church. We quickly found a community that embraced us and a walk with God that had not been part of our relationship thus far, though we both were raised in church.

It was in that community I found myself in a sort of unofficial mentorship with a brother many years my senior. He would often check in with me, offer counsel, and sometimes even give a little correction.

We found ourselves sitting on the patio of the lodge at a men's retreat one year. We talked about growing up. His childhood was a lot like mine. We lamented things we wished we had done differently. Having given thought to the years of violence, anger, and keeping God at arm's length, I asked him, "How does a man atone for such an ugly life?"

His response? "With the one that you still have." That advice was offered in such an effortless way. He didn't even need to give the question any thought. It was advice he had also received many years prior, and it had become something that encouraged him.

It showed in the way he lived, how he interacted with people, and the kindness he exudes even today.

Since then, I've made it my goal to give back more, to fill the hole I created in the world with goodness.

The movie *The Forge* has a great line that has always stuck with me: "It is better to be a fountain than a drain." Don't you just love that?

How does a man wipe his life clean? With the one he has.

Stepping Into God's Presence

Sense His presence in everyday moments and divine interventions

Divine Intervention

Jordan Ramos

"Moses answered the people, 'Do not be afraid. Stand firm and you will see the deliverance the Lord will bring you today. The Egyptians you see today you will never see again. The Lord will fight for you; you need only to be still."
-Exodus 14:13-14

As a young adult, my husband worked for a local trucking company in Guatemala City. It was not always the safest of jobs, so teams usually traveled together. One evening, he was parked on the side of the road while his coworkers left for home. He stayed behind so he could watch over the truck. As he sat comfortably and unguarded in the driver's seat, the door swung open. He suddenly felt a hand grab him by the neck of his shirt and yank him out of the truck. It was the cartel.

The team of men worked together to steal the truck, tie my husband up, and drag him to a nearby forest out of sight. As he felt the cold nuzzle of the gun press against his head, he trembled with fear. Moments of his life flashed by. But the trigger wasn't pulled. After a while, he was set free. How could this happen? The cartel is not in the business of setting people free, especially when a victim can identify them. It was God's divine intervention. The Lord saved my husband that day.

My husband's story reminds me of the Israelites fleeing from Pharaoh. They were terrified because they had no visible path before them. My husband had no visible path before him. Yet the sea was parted, and the Israelites walked on solid ground. The cartel had a miraculous change of heart and set my husband free. God's supernatural intervention saved the victims in both stories. His will was not finished for His people.

God has many names, but the two that stand out to me in these stories are Jehovah Jireh, meaning "our provider," and Jehovah Mephalti, meaning "deliverer." He provides protection when we need it and delivers us from impossible circumstances. What do you need protection or deliverance from?

Lord, I thank You for Your protection and deliverance. I ask You to protect me from _____ and to deliver me from _____. Help me to trust You wholeheartedly in the midst of what seems impossible. I believe in Your divine intervention, and I am taking a step in faith to give up any control I hold on to. I choose to rest in Your divine presence, knowing Your will for my life continues writing the story. Help me to stand firm in Your presence and rest in Your peace. In Jesus' name I pray. Amen.

Fearing the Unknown

Niki Barlow

"So do not fear, for I am with you; do not be dismayed, for I am your God. I will strengthen you and help you; I will uphold you with my righteous right hand."
-Isaiah 41:10

Leaving my husband's pastoral job with two foster children in tow was not an easy decision. We were on an extended trip, looking for a new place to winter where my husband could continue to heal after a death-defying motorcycle accident. He had mended quite a bit, but his broken bones, internal bleeding, and blunt force trauma still caused pain and breathing problems. His immune system was weak, which left him vulnerable to viruses.

We traveled through Texas, New Mexico, and Arizona in our fifth wheel. As we left South Padre Island, my husband was not feeling well. Continuing our journey, he became confused. Not sure what was going on, he went to an urgent care where he was told there was nothing wrong with him. At one stop, he vomited so violently the camp staff even noticed. Many miles later, we landed in Tucson, Arizona. After two more urgent care stops and a late-night trip to the emergency room, no one understood what was happening, but they gave him an inhaler and some antibiotics.

We feared it could be COVID, a new disease doctors did not understand but was killing many. Since my husband had no sore throat, they eliminated COVID as a possibility. In some ways, I'm glad. I could nurse my husband. He never had to be hospitalized. Isolation from family and friends was common during this time as medical staff dealt with trying to contain COVID. We later learned there was an outbreak of the disease in San Antonio while we were there. He did have COVID. Fortunately, no one else got it from him.

In the middle of the night, when he clung to me, shivering, delirious from fever, my hopes and fears were placed before God through prayer. There were no easy fixes. I was scared as I watched him suffer. The motorcycle accident had been incredibly hard as we faced his injuries, but we had CT scans and tests to inform us what was going on with his body. This debilitating disease had no answer. Several times, I wondered if he would live through the night. During those dark days, I leaned on God to hold my hand and watch over us one moment at a time.

God's provision comes in many ways. He helped us when school was canceled the day before we were to leave for our Colorado home. Staying at our campground provided activities for the kids and sunny, dry days to aid in my husband's recuperation. After six weeks, he gradually got better.

When you are amid a time of terror, remember that you are never alone. Take refuge in God's presence. Call out to Him, giving Him your worries. When human knowledge has no answers, He will comfort you and guide you.

Feasting Our Faith with Prayer

Greg Grandchamp

"In the same way, the Spirit helps us in our weakness. We do not know what we ought to pray for, but the Spirit himself intercedes for us through wordless groans. And he who searches our hearts knows the mind of the Spirit, because the Spirit intercedes for God's people in accordance with the will of God."
-Romans 8:26-27

A good prayer life can be difficult after finding time with the kids, work, events, cooking meals, and keeping up the house. You're already up early, and by the time the day ends, you fall into bed exhausted or simply turn on the TV and watch like a zombie. Let's face it: Life is busy and can feel like a train wreck. Sometimes it actually is a train wreck—filled with pain and chaos—and you don't know how to get out of it.

Oh sure, you still pray—when something goes wrong or you need help with something. Often (too often) your prayers are formal and meaningless. Empty. But let's be real: We both know that isn't what a good prayer life is all about.

Don't think you know how to pray? Sit down alone and tell God that. Tell Him about your challenges. Tell Him what is hurting your heart. And tell Him about your joys. Thank Him for opening your heart to Him—and for opening your eyes to your spiritual drift and saving you from it. Tell him you need Him in your life. More than that, you need Him to lead you. Tell Him that you want nothing more—and nothing less—than to be in His will, not your own. And if this isn't what you want, ask Him to help you to want it.

If you pursue Him with your whole heart, you will find Him. Nothing—and I do mean nothing—will keep God from pursuing you. You are His beloved child, and His love for you is everlasting. But maybe take a few minutes away from social media, television, or wherever it is you spend your downtime. Trust me, it will be worth it.

Ask Him to help you trust. Ask these things every day. Every. Single. Day.

Father in heaven, You already know that I have been struggling to come to You in prayer. You already know that I am desperate and don't even have the words to speak to You now. Please touch my heart. Please let me feel Your presence and Your forgiveness once more. Amen.

God Shows Up in Big Ways

Jordan Ramos

*"Ask and it will be given to you; seek and you will find; knock
and the door will be opened to you. For everyone who asks
receives; the one who seeks finds; and to the one who knocks, the
door will be opened."*
-Matthew 7:7-8

It was a warm spring afternoon when my roommate invited
several of her friends and family members over to our townhouse for a
barbecue. The house was crammed with people, and yet as I stood in
the middle of the room I felt completely alone. It was in this season of
life where I spent many of my prayers asking for a godly husband. Like
many of us do, I struggled with loneliness.

It was during this time when God began to place a desire on
my heart to bring my younger sister on a mission trip to Guatemala.
The week I was there, I had an unexpected interview for a teaching
position, and within two months I had moved. Little did I know I
would meet the love of my life within two months of living there. God
led me 2,528 miles to my husband and filled the loneliness in my life
and the missing piece in my heart. He orchestrated every detail, both
large and small.

God will guide us toward and through the plans He has for us, but we have to be willing to listen and follow. In doing so, not only will God answer, but He will do more than we can imagine. Not only did He answer my many prayers, but He healed my heart and strengthened our relationship in the process. He wants our vulnerability, trust, and complete dependence. I do not know the struggles you face today, but I do know He hears you. Continue to pray and rely on Him. Matthew 7:7-8 promises us God is listening; you will find Him, and He will provide. If you feel a pull on your heart, follow it and watch how God shows up in big ways.

Dear Lord, I thank You for listening to my prayers, opening the door when I knock, and providing when I ask. Lord, please place a desire on my heart that You want me to follow. Continue to give me a renewal of strength and peace as I seek You. I trust You and know You will show up in big ways. In Jesus' name I pray. Amen.

Prayer Rock

Trudy Hewitt

"For since the creation of the world God's invisible qualities—his eternal power and divine nature—have been clearly seen, being understood from what has been made, so that people are without excuse."
-Romans 1:20

This morning, as I sat on my prayer rock thinking about the Lord, there was a chipmunk sitting on a rock near me. He was almost perfectly camouflaged, so much so that my dog ran right past him. The chippie just sat there and looked out at the dog. I wondered if he was thinking: "stupid dog." I looked at the trees and at a bunny walking by. I looked at the bushes and the grass, and I looked up at the sky. The sky was like a bunch of little cotton balls with bits of deep blue peeking in between. I was thinking about how God made all kinds of different clouds, what fun He must have had doing that, and how He must enjoy them as I'm enjoying them. And I'm living here on this earth—how could that be by some kind of cosmic accident? And I'm watching my dog, an awesome and loving creature, and wondering how that could happen by an accident. I don't see how anyone could even believe that because I can hardly believe that I'm sitting here on this rock, looking at these clouds in the sky and this landscape and the dog and the bunny and the chipmunk in the rocks, and my arms and my legs work—***and* I** have a God who loves me and cares for me and a family who loves me. I can hardly believe the full enormity of my life.

The whole thing rather overwhelms me. I spent time talking to God about how I got here, how I have survived this long, and why He made me as He did. I always take time to praise Him for who He is, and today I praise Him for how He made this world and how He made me. I am in what they call the twilight of my life. I have far more yesterdays than tomorrows. That does not bother me. Life does not bother me. My life is peace. I live in a world with a pandemic, lots of viruses, race riots, and political unrest.

I lived through race riots and political unrest in the 1960s. This is a rewind for me. I lived through Vietnam, when many of my friends were going off to war and then some didn't return. So, my prayer rock has also become a constant. So many days the sun shines on it and warms my body as it warms my soul. Many days it is covered with snow, and on those days, I sit inside and look out at God's creation. Still, He warms my soul.

But the one overriding constant in my life has been my God. He never changed. He never left me. He never moved. I have moved. I have grown closer to Him. And the closer I've grown, the more I survived this life in peace.

Oh Lord, my God, I praise You for Your wonderful blessings, Your love, and Your divine nature. Thank You for who You are. Thank You for being a constant in my life. Amen.

Pressing Past the Pain Into His Presence

Kirsten Wegele

"But as for me, it is good to be near God. I have made the Sovereign Lord my refuge; I will tell of all your deeds."
-Psalm 73:28

The times we feel the most pain are the times that we need to press the most into God. Just reminiscing on the things of the past while lying in bed one night, I began to "continue" to write my story of where God has brought me, my husband, and our family in the last few years. I can't help but think that God is watching over us and thinking, "I'm *so* proud of you!" It's been in some of the darkest moments that we as a family *still* praised Him. We *still* sought after Him with purpose and passion to lean into His love.

We looked past and did not understand certain situations we had been through, whether they were self-inflicted pains of the past or just what life had thrown at us that year. But we continued to look into the eyes of a loving Father who is *always good* and *always faithful*. Some may not have been able to see His goodness in the midst of the circumstances that we had been tried through, but we *did*, and we *still* do!

You see, I have experienced too much in my walk to not believe that He is good. Our God is a God who wants us to passionately pursue Him. It's not based off of feeling as though I have to praise Him, but off of a love and heart to know that He is infinitely worthy of being praised. It is about knowing that He *always* will contend for us! He is, above all else, worthy of our praise.

It's in the times that we feel the most pain that we can experience His presence, and, in His presence, we are filled with peace. It's a peace that surpasses all of our own understanding and continually leads us back to His heart.

Today I pray that you can press past the pain into His presence, into the presence of a greater God where His goodness overflows with love being poured out on you, on your heart, and on the situation that lies in front of you. I pray that you will have eyes to see like He sees and ears to hear His voice gently speaking truth over you. Seek Him in all things as you go forth this week. James 4:8 (ESV) says, "Draw near to God, and He will draw near to you."

Self-Reflection

Bobbie Bomar Brown

"Therefore, there is now no condemnation for those who are in Christ Jesus, because through Christ Jesus the law of the Spirit who gives life has set you free from the law of sin and death."
-Romans 8:1-2

My two-year-old son loved all the superheroes. The Superman Halloween costume, complete with a mask, was a perfect fit for him.

As we were opening the wooden door to venture out to trick our neighbors, hoping that delicious chocolate candy would be dropped into his orange plastic pumpkin, a little Superman boy was staring back at us. It startled my son, and he didn't want to continue his adventure of running door-to-door. It took several minutes before his dad could convince him there wasn't anything to fear. He was only seeing his reflection in the glass door.

The night ended with the kids spreading their treats across the floor, choosing the ones they wanted and discarding the others. Of course, they gave their mom her favorites.

This story made me reflect on how we put our masks on before venturing out of our home to gain favor from others, often by trickery, choosing one moral and discarding others.

My son chose the Superman costume because the TV was his guidepost. He believed the message that all he had to do was wear the Superman mask and he would have great powers. However, when his dad explained he was only seeing his own reflection of himself, my son's fear left. He trusted his dad for guidance.

Are we listening to our heavenly Father enough to know that the masks we wear hold no superpowers and that it is safe to remove the masks and be honest with ourselves? Can we face the truth and realize that often our masks are used to trick people into receiving a treat? Let's ask ourselves who is influencing our costumes.

Our external masks do not define us, although we often allow them to influence us. We can hide, blame, or live controlled by our choices, but the message from our heavenly Father is clear: We have nothing to fear. He doesn't see us as blurry or broken reflections. Our identity comes from Christ. Allow God to be your guidepost.

Father, I pray we can always look at our reflection and that it only honors You when we open the door to venture out or remain in the confines of our home. I pray that if the reflection staring back at me scares me, I quickly call Your name and ask for Your truth and Your reminder the Bible is my guidepost, not the world. Amen.

Teach the Children

Karren Mitchell

"...Teach them to your children and to their children after them."
-Deuteronomy 4:9

I have always been interested in stories about my family. Some of my fondest memories are of the times I'd plant myself next to my father on my grandfather's porch and listen to stories about "the good old days."

Many of those family stories influenced which version of the Bible I preferred. I prefer the King James Version of the Bible. But why I prefer it is the story. The new version is easier to understand, but the King James Version was the version so many of my ancestors read, memorized, and preached from.

My great-grandfather was a circuit-riding Methodist minister in the 1880s in Missouri. I have his Bible. All my ancestors' names are meticulously recorded in his handwriting in that Bible. It is the King James Version. How could I not love that relic of the past?

Then there is the story of my great-grandmother who lived in Caney, Kansas. She was a feisty woman who planted a victory garden and sent her son off to World War I to fight in France. The day she sent her son off to the Army was the last day she spoke German. She swore that if the kaiser was going to shoot at her son, she would never speak German again. She was true to her words. I have nothing from her written in German. There were no relics from her side of the family that indicate she ever even spoke German.

I do have the stories my father's sister shared with me about this remarkable woman that everyone called Ma.

Ma's house was always filled with children, and she loved reading stories to them from the Bible. She would gather the children around her big wooden rocking chair in her rose garden with her golden retriever, Shep, at her feet and read to the children.

She would read stories from the Old and New Testament, then end her reading by saying, "Thus saieth the Lord," or John, Luke, or whichever book she'd just read.

In those days, there was a monthly magazine called *Comfort*. In each issue, there would be a story for children about a mischievous bear named Cubby. When the magazine arrived in the mail, she'd gather the children around and read the adventures of Cubby, ending the story with, "Thus saieth Cubby Bear."

The stories shared with me as a child have influenced me throughout my life. They have driven me to find answers to questions, and they have fostered a love of Bible stories.

Whatever version of the Bible you choose, share those stories with your children. You will be sharing it with many generations, not just the one.

Beauty From Ashes

See beauty rise from
ashes, as He redeems
loss into new purpose

Checking the Currency in Our Testimony

Kirsten Wegele

"When you have eaten and are satisfied, praise the Lord your God for the good land he has given you. Be careful that you do not forget the Lord your God, failing to observe his commands, his laws and his decrees that I am giving you this day."
-Deuteronomy 8:10-11

But Titus. Those were the words that the Lord spoke to me when I would stand in doubt and allow the questions to lead to unbelief. We had had two more second trimester miscarriages without any answers, and my heart was deeply wounded. The enemy wanted to make death as uncomfortable as possible for me. He wanted me to feel so vulnerable and defeated with death that it would cause confusion and doubt and lead me to questions for which I didn't have answers. I would sit and wonder, "Why did this happen to me yet again?" With that question of *why*, my heart would start to doubt God.

But Titus, God would gently whisper to me. This was the best reminder I have ever received in life. **But Titus!** It's because he was the last baby I had that the enemy almost tried to take, **but God**. God worked miracles in his life and breathed life into a baby who only took one breath and then went limp. It's God who healed him of a skeletal disorder that the doctors said he'd have for the rest of his life. **But God**. God overabundantly continues to show up. Each time my mind starts to wonder and get stuck, that simple **But Titus** reminds me of His goodness in every situation I have been through. It's like those words in the song "Goodness of God": "All my life You have been faithful; all my life you have been so, so good."

I want to remind you today that we cannot fail to forget what God has done in our lives and in the lives of others. What is your "but God" moment? What have you seen in your life or in someone else's life that needs to be shared as a reminder of testimony? I believe we are always to be checking the currency of our situations. You are probably asking, "What does that mean?" I mean that in every circumstance that we go through, we have the opportunity (yes, it's a choice) to *choose* to remember. We can remember the bad and the ugly of the situation—or we can choose to look at even the littlest thing that God did in that moment.

If you look back on your life, I'm sure you could see at least one thing that God did now that you're out of that certain situation. Seek Him and remember what He's done. Check the currency of past or current situations and dwell on what He can do!

"At this I fell at His feet to worship Him. But He said to me, 'Don't do that! I am a fellow servant with you and with your brothers and sisters who hold to the testimony of Jesus. Worship God! For it is the Spirit of prophecy who bears testimony to Jesus'" (Revelation 19:10).

Forgiveness Not Returned

Joe Pierce

"Jesus said, 'Father, forgive them, for they do not know what they are doing"
-Luke 23:34

We all know this verse. You may not be able to quote the chapter and verse, but you can certainly quote the text. In that moment, Jesus taught His last and perhaps one of His greatest lessons: forgiveness in the middle of pain. More importantly, forgiving when the other party isn't interested in receiving it or isn't even able to acknowledge any fault.

The people who hung Jesus on the cross didn't care that He forgave them. Maybe those who have hurt you don't either. Author Lawana Blackwell said, "Forgiveness is almost a selfish act because of its immense benefits to the one who forgives."

When we forgive without expectations, we release those who have injured us. We are not just releasing them; we are also setting ourselves free—free from the anger, free from the pain that was inflicted, free from the weight of carrying that burden.

God gives us freedom; we can lay our burdens on Him. We can turn that offense over to Him.

"Do not repay evil with evil or insult with insult. On the contrary, repay evil with blessing, because to this you were called so that you may inherit a blessing (1 Peter 3:9).

Forgiveness feels easier when someone says, "I'm sorry." When there's recognition, repentance, and remorse, it can make healing seem like a possibility. But what about when none of that comes? When the person who hurts you does not acknowledge it—or worse, doesn't care?

Jesus understands that pain.

Forgiving without receiving it in return doesn't mean pretending you are not hurt. It doesn't mean excusing what was done. It means making the choice to release the offense into God's hands and letting Him carry the weight.

This kind of forgiveness doesn't indicate weakness; it shows strength. It means putting trust in the fact that God sees the full story and will deal with it justly, even when others don't. It's choosing peace over being bitter. It means healing over hardness. Forgiveness protects your heart; without it, your heart grows hard.

You may never get the apology, but through Christ, you can get freedom. ***So, let it go!*** We don't have the power to change anything that falls to God. Forgive and pray for them. Lift them up and pray God would meet them where they are. What would it look like to release that hurt to God today? It looks like freedom.

Lord, You know my heart and the hurt that I feel. I choose to forgive, even without an apology. Help me release the anger and offense into Your hands and walk in the freedom You offer. Teach me to love like You. Amen.

The Annunciation

Millie Carpenter

*"But the angel said to her, 'Do not be afraid, Mary; you have
found favor with God.'... 'I am the Lord's servant,' Mary
answered. 'May your word to me be fulfilled.'"*
-Luke 1:30, 38

In the stuffy attic classroom of my college art building, tapping
my foot on the stained carpet and doodling notes, my heart paused
when the professor flicked Leonardo da Vinci's *The Annunciation* onto
the display.

Over the past year, I had experienced personal grief and loss
beyond what I had previously imagined possible. My existence felt like
a cry to God of desperation, weakness, and confusion on a perpetual
loop. Some days, the cry was on the forefront of my heart, spilling out
the corners of my eyes in classes and simple conversations. Other days,
it sapped my strength in a subtle, steady stream that was easier to
ignore.

Suddenly, the pain paused. Flowers and robes spilled onto the
ground around Leonardo da Vinci's angel, his halo a spiky ray of gold
that gilded his hawklike wings. His soft eyes lifted, brow bent, fingers
dipping toward Mary in blessing. A question entered my on-pause
heart: If God were to make an annunciation to me declaring what He
asks of me today, what would He say? What would He be asking of

me? Would I be able to see that call, like Mary, as a blessing and a strength, despite the difficulty?

In the lily clutched in the painted angel's hands, God spoke—what He calls me to He also blesses me with the strength for. I do not drink this cup alone. He asks that I drink this cup with Him, but He is drinking with me too. The cup of grief. The cup of suffering, loss, aching, violence, or pain. And here, in our day's annunciation, God invites us to let go of our grasping fear of tomorrow—can we be resilient? Will we still love others when we are weighed down by pain? Will we lose trust in the One who has held us all this way?

The very next thing He calls us to is simply to say yes. To say yes, maybe to joyful tasks, maybe to sowing in tears, but always with the confidence that He is both with us and blessing us as He calls us.

Suffering Christ, You know and see the ways our days bleed with pains and fears that crush us and steal our strength. Help us know the constancy of Your presence and the relief of Your promise to drink this cup with us. Revive us when we sow in tears and help us to answer yes to Your call, even when we cannot yet see Your extended strength and blessing. Amen.

The Lord Is My Shepherd

Karren Mitchell

"Even though I walk through the darkest valley, I will fear no evil, for you are with me; your rod and your staff, they comfort me."

−Psalm 23:4

I don't know how many times I have said this verse from the Psalms. Every time I've been afraid, I have said it, whispered it, or thought it.

In 2020, the world closed down due to the COVID pandemic, and every day was a day filled with fear: fear for myself, fear for my family who were essential workers, and fear for health care workers who were on the front line of this war against an insidious and invisible enemy.

This was a terrible time. I lost family and friends to this dreaded killer. Alone in my home, a cocoon of safety, I wondered what I could do to help. The first shortages the world experienced were of protective gear. My family members were tying bandanas around their faces when they had to go out into the world. I was a quilter, and like most quilters, I had a massive fabric stash. Quilters' stashes are even more unique than just a miscellaneous collection of fabric. Our stashes are one hundred percent cotton, the perfect fabric for masks.

I made masks for my family and for the teachers who were caring for my granddaughter each day and who had no masks. I sent masks to my cousins in the Midwest, and they, in turn, sent me some spare elastic and bias tape so that I could make more masks.

I made almost 200 masks, and each day I prayed. I memorized the 23rd Psalm, probably just from repeating it so often. I prayed for myself, for my family, and for the world. I also focused on my health by exercising and dieting. If I survived, I wanted to be able to be part of the world again.

I grew more spiritual during this time of crisis. I started attending devotionals online using the new communication tool Zoom. That was a godsend during that time. I kept in touch with my family and friends. For my baby granddaughter, I recorded songs and stories so she wouldn't forget who I was. And I waited.

I formed some good habits during this time, and I loved Zoom. The pandemic has passed, but I still use Zoom for meetings, devotionals, book clubs, and writing groups. When I go out into the world, I still wear a mask, but I treasure the fact that I can go out into the world by myself and interact with others.

Join me each night before you go to sleep and pray Psalm 23 with me. The world can be a dangerous place, but the words of Psalms provide comfort and calm.

Till Death We Didn't Part...

Joe Pierce

*"And provide for those who grieve in Zion—to bestow on them a
crown of beauty instead of ashes, the oil of joy instead of
mourning, and a garment of praise instead of a spirit of despair.
They will be called oaks of righteousness, a planting of the Lord
for the display of his splendor."*
-Isaiah 61:3

We knew God as kids and began dating during our senior year
of high school. By our early twenties, we were married and not walking
with God. By our 9th year of marriage, we had split.

Not only did God renew our love a year later, but He also led
us back to Him and to the community of believers that we would "do
life with."

God expanded our family with three additional kids and gave
us the best years of our marriage. It was then that God saved my life
and renewed my health through a very large weight loss. ***He*** was
equipping me for my greatest trial.

Just after her 46th birthday, my wife would get the call you
never expect. The doctor needed to see her first thing Monday
morning—it was Friday afternoon at the time.

She was diagnosed with stage three esophageal cancer, a cancer
that wasn't supposed to attack 46-year-old women. We had God, and
we were ready for war!

Chemo and radiation knocked her into the dirt. There were times she was too weak to walk to the bathroom to be sick. There were countless hospital stays. When I couldn't be there, two very dear friends would stay with her. I worked and did my best to still be Dad.

Sadly, a lot of people were absent during this time. That was so hard to watch. During this period, she prayed, not for healing, but for those she loved, for the hearts of those who struggled to watch her suffer.

As her body failed, God drew her closer each day. She embraced this verse: "Though he slay me, yet will I hope in him…" (Job 13:15).

It is an indescribable thing to stand alongside your children as they say goodbye to their mother. It was my lowest point. With family and friends gathered around her bed, I walked her home for the final time. We learned much from each other over the years. Having faith amidst her greatest pain was the last thing she would teach me.

God had more than equipped me for this next chapter. He blessed me with strength and healing. He didn't take away the pain and grief; He just offered to carry it.

My faith is stronger today than ever. God blessed me and my children with not just another amazing woman of God that He chose for me and my kids, but another son and brother who himself had lost his dad a year prior to us losing my wife. God gathered our broken threads and knitted a beautifully blended new tapestry and future together with Him at the center.

We are called to suffer as Christians:

"Not only so, but we also glory in our sufferings, because we know that suffering produces perseverance; perseverance, character; and character, hope. And hope does not put us to shame, because God's love has been poured out into our hearts through the Holy Spirit, who has been given to us" (Romans 5:3-5).

Pray: Father, please comfort me as I weather this storm in my life. I know that even this hard season is a blessing. Give me strength and patience as You reveal Your plan for my life.

Turning Adversity Into Hope

Debra Hill-Gray

"Not only so, but we also glory in our sufferings, because we know that suffering produces perseverance; perseverance, character; and character, hope."
-Romans 5:3-4

The words my friend spoke to me that warm August night upon observing my son returning from work—sweat racing down his face, hands shaky, and a tone inflection unrecognizable by me—resonate with me still: "Your son is on heroin!" I recall the audacity of her claim. Even remembering she'd experienced it with her child, how could she say this about mine? Yet I knew something was terribly wrong. Weeks passed before I confirmed her words to be true.

How could my child be using such a nasty drug? My child wasn't "one of them," I thought, as reality set in. I knew nothing about hard drugs. I thought only bad people did them. My son wasn't bad! That was my uneducated, judgmental thought process. As other family members learned of his addiction, judgment abounded from all. I was devastated, left to fight this battle alone. My only hope was in God's promise: *"...Never will I leave you; never will I forsake you"* (Hebrews 13:5).

My ungodly judgment evolved into understanding and compassion as I dived into learning everything possible about the disease of addiction. I felt my hopelessness turn to perseverance, determined not to allow my child to die from a disease he didn't understand.

When he returned from inpatient rehabilitation, I'd already begun my journey of building a social media page offering resources, inspiration, and hope for others struggling with addiction and their loved ones. Two decades later, I find myself stronger in my passion for helping others, knowing they should never have to experience the loneliness and hopelessness we endured. Everyone from all walks of life deserves someone to guide them through those same uncharted waters we once navigated alone. My hope remains that those lost in their downward journey will see God's light in me and begin their journey to recovery.

Recently, I said to my son, "I'm sorry you had to go through such a painful journey." He replied, "Mom, my addiction happened so God could equip you to help the many people you have." It was then I realized that God had used his addiction to give me strength, endurance, and perseverance to guide others towards healing too.

Father, help us use our struggles as beacons of Your light, shining through our hearts, allowing others to see You working through us. Help us always turn our adversities into perseverance, good character, and hope for others, with all the glory to You.

Victory from Tragedy

Trudy Hewitt

"This is the victory that has overcome the world, even our faith."
-1 John 5:4

Our youth group was on a trip from Broomfield, Colorado, to Monterey, California, in the early 1990s. Chris was supposed to be with us, even though her family had recently moved to Southern California. The day before she was to join us, she drove with her father to Phoenix to rescue her brother's Mustang and return it to SoCal.

After arriving in Phoenix, they turned right around and started back, but Chris fell asleep at the wheel. She veered off the road and, as the Mustang crashed into large rocks, she was pushed into the back seat. A small compressed air tank in the back seat collided with her head. She was declared dead at the scene, but a nurse stopped and administered CPR, saving her life.

The nurse was on the way to work in Palm Springs at one of the best trauma centers in the country. Chris was airlifted there, where her saga began. She had a closed head injury, and her brain was swollen. The trauma doctor performed another lifesaving procedure and removed her skull from the right half of her brain, leaving it open to air and airborne infections. She was in a coma for several weeks.

In the meantime, our youth group arrived in Monterey. Parents told our kids, who were obviously very upset. I cancelled activities at our conference that day, and we went to the beach, sat in a circle, and prayed.

The impact of this tragedy on our kids was unbelievable. God moved among them in many ways. They were all convicted of His power, His love, and His ability to save Chris, and we had many heartfelt prayer times as a group during that youth conference.

Seven weeks later, Chris awoke. Doctors asked her questions, and she gave them her name, her new address, and other accurate information. Her brain was intact. She was paralyzed, but her spunk remained unchanged. She received a cardboard alphabet covered in plastic wrap, and she would tap letters to communicate. I realized quickly that she was tapping words to make fun of *me*!

God used this tragedy to touch many of our kids, who made commitments to ministry that week and in ensuing visits with Chris.

If tragedy enters your life, I encourage you, too, to turn first to God. Learn what lessons He might have for you.

Father, I trust you. As I sit here in worry and fear, I hand them to You. Show me Your way. Amen.

When the Rivers Rage

Niki Barlow

*"When you pass through the waters, I will be with you; and when
you pass through the rivers, they will not sweep over you. When
you walk through the fire, you will not be burned; the flames will
not set you ablaze."*
-Isaiah 43:2

Three days of drizzling rain moved into a torrential downpour.
I laid my head down. The raindrops were a constant rhythm helping
me drift off to sleep. The next day would be another soggy one. Late
that night, the phone started to ring, never a good sign. Our neighbor
called to tell us the police department was trying to wake us. My
husband scrambled up and headed for the door.

Our neighborhood was a raging river. The road was gone, and
we were being evacuated. We would have to hike up our backyard hill
to get out. Being one of the highest houses on our cul-de-sac allowed
us to stay, becoming a haven for our neighbor as well. We watched as
the river crept closer to our house, one foot after another. The
neighbor's house had water rushing through it, but the house remained
standing.

When the sun rose the next day, our closest bridge went out, funneling most of the water away. Still, smaller steady streams continued running down our street. This began a long journey of shoveling sand, moving furniture for our neighbors, and praying. We went without electricity, water, gas, sewer, and cell service for days. Evacuation centers opened. We waited in line to call our children to let them know we were OK. Portable toilets popped up in every neighborhood.

We were blessed to have a camper on higher ground, and we moved that into a church parking lot. Eventually, my husband, a pastor, worked with our church to become the lead in organizing teams to come help. We served the volunteers meals, took the teams to different locations, assessed needs, and prayed with them.

Our faith grew as we helped and encouraged neighbors, our city, and surrounding towns affected by the flood. God used us to speak and live out our belief in Jesus. Every step we took was given to God. We prayed for unity with Him. As the years went by, houses, roads, and bridges were repaired, removed, or cleaned up, but the most important work done was sharing God's love.

Father, thank You for supporting us through the devastation of loss. We did not lose life, but we gained eternal perspective and fellow followers. When the rivers rage, help us to see You holding the lifeline so that we do not get swept away, but instead teach us to thrive and feel Your holy presence. Amen.

Meet the Authors

Niki Barlow is an author, blogger, and child advocate. She and her husband, retired Pastor Richard, raised a blended family of seven children in Estes Park, Colorado. She now lives in Loveland, Colorado, where she enjoys beautiful sunsets, snowy mountaintops, and hot tea by the fireplace. She loves a variety of musical styles but cannot carry a tune!

Traveling, writing, and hanging out with her six grandbabies are favorite pastimes.

No stranger to unexpected challenges, discouragement, brokenness, or adversities, Niki has found true joy through God's grace. She has experienced firsthand God's plan to overcome and redeem even when it did not appear possible.

Niki's books can be found on Amazon, including *Fostering the Heart* devotionals and the *Sharing with God* journal. Join her at **www.fosteringtheheart.com** and sign up for her newsletter. The Fostering the Heart website is where you will find encouragement, devotionals, blog posts, and her husband, Richard's, wedding and marriage counseling services.

Bobbie Bomar Brown, a Texas native, now calls Colorado home, where she resides with her husband, Mike, and their two adopted cats, Monty and Milo.

Bobbie's writing draws on her personal experiences and tragedies and illuminates the power of faith and love.

In her first book, *The Unbreakable Cord*, she shares the horrific details of the car accident caused by a drunk driver that nearly took her daughter's life—missing the spinal cord by less than a millimeter.

Shattered Not Broken: A Mother's Journey Through Her Daughter's Car Accident and Her Son's Suicide, released in early 2025 on Amazon. Written as a parallel narrative, it recounts her daughter's life-changing injuries and celebrates her recovery. Bobbie uses her love of cooking and collecting recipes to work through the grief of her son's suicide. The inclusion of his poems, family stories, and recipes adds a personal touch, providing a break from the intense narrative.

Bobbie believes beauty can come out of the ashes and continues to write devotions to heal and grow with God.

Millie Carpenter is a Colorado native, earning a bachelor's degree in international affairs and Spanish at Berry College in Rome, Georgia, after several years of working in ministry. She writes about life, theology, and her travel experiences.

Millie is passionate about theology that is rooted in daily realities and pushes us into a deeper community with God and our neighbors. Inspired by a long line of faithful everyday women who contributed to her faith and by female theologians, Millie looks forward to finding ways to share her faith in her writing, build up the lives of other young women, and invest in her community.

A member of the Women of Welcome community, Millie is learning new ways to pursue compassion and promote Christlike hospitality throughout the United States and in her local neighborhood. Millie writes on Substack @milliecarpenter.

Dr. Katie Erickson grew up in Dearborn, Michigan, but has lived in Findlay, Ohio, since 2007. After earning a bachelor's degree in electrical engineering from Ohio Northern University, she earned her master of divinity and doctor of ministry degrees (with a focus on Biblical Hebrew) from Winebrenner Theological Seminary in Findlay, Ohio.

Katie has a passion for teaching, especially regarding the Biblical Hebrew language and anything to do with the Bible. Having "retired" from engineering in 2020, she now works with three different ministries, helps authors publish books (and has published seven of her own books), manages her rental properties, teaches at the seminary, and does a variety of other things that make life interesting and fun. Check out her website at KatieEricksonEditing.com.

Greg Grandchamp and his wife of 40 years live in a small town in northern Colorado. Greg grew up in New England but spent most of his life in California, including raising his family in the Glendale area, moving to Colorado over 20 years ago.

Greg grew up Catholic and always "believed" in God and in Jesus, but it meant nothing in his life. He was one of many "cultural Christians" who knew about Jesus, but didn't know Jesus. He had no personal relationship with Jesus and didn't live his faith—yet always felt a draw on his heart. This is why Greg writes about what it means to live out our faith in our daily lives. To live as we are called by the teaching of Jesus. To build our lives on rock and not on sand.

After a more than 45-year career in mortgage lending, Greg has been a contributing writer for Christianity.com and BibleStudyTools.com. He also published a book titled *In Pursuit of Truth: A Journey Begins*, available on Amazon.

Debra Hill-Gray discovered her love for writing in high school, dreaming of becoming a journalist. While life led her in a different direction, she continued writing occasional blogs, devotionals, and technical policies and procedures during her career in corporate America.

Debbie's personal hardships with loved ones struggling with addiction shifted her career to substance use disorder. Although now retired, you'll still find her advocating for people and their families today while also managing her informative Facebook page, Drug/Alcohol Addiction, Recovery, and Family Support.

Debbie enjoys her time being an independent Scentsy consultant, traveling, reading, beach therapy, and most of all, spending time with her family and grandchildren, the lights of her life!

Debbie is no stranger to loss. Besides losing two stillborn daughters in her early 20s, she lost two sisters in 1999 and 2000 to cancer. This was an especially difficult time for Debbie after losing her mother just one month prior to losing her first sister.

Trudy Hewitt would often be asked where she grew up, and she would chuckle and say, "Kansas, Missouri, New Mexico, and California." After she let that sink in, she would wait. If they wanted to know more, Trudy explained she grew up in a 48' by 8' house trailer. Her dad could get a job and go to work instantly, so they moved sometimes two or three times a year, with maybe 15 minutes' notice.

The theme of the book she is currently writing is called *Trailer Trash*. Her *Read to Me Mommy* series is a collection of children's books.

She trusts God to direct her life and has grown with Him so much over the years. Sharing devotions is so fun for her as she loves and worships God all the time.

Trudy has been writing pretty much all her life. She has been published in *Group* magazine and as a contributing author in several Group Publishing books. She is an editor and loves that, but currently, she is writing three books. As a worship leader in two churches, Trudy loves sharing these devotions.

Karren Mitchell was raised in Kingman, Arizona, and attended Northern Arizona University. She is a retired elementary school teacher who specializes in computer science and gifted and talented instruction. She has a master's degree in curriculum development and administration.

Karren has written two family histories and ghostwritten an autobiography as well as two children's books and numerous science fiction stories. Her artwork has earned several awards.

She loves genealogy, art, quilting, music, reading, and writing. She participates in several religious and writing groups each week on Zoom and frequently teaches children's art classes.

Karren lives with her family in Riverside, California. She is currently working on her first science fiction novel and another family history, *The Mitchell Family in Indiana, Kentucky, and Missouri.*

Shelby Perryman attended Capernwray Bible School in Quebec. She is a wife and mother of two children. Just getting started on her writing journey, her life is filled with kids' sports, and she is an avid Kansas City Chiefs football fan.

Joe Pierce was born and grew up in Nashville, Tennessee. He moved to Mesa, Arizona, in late 1995 with his late wife, Kim, who he met during their senior year of high school. Married for nearly twenty-four years, they had four kids: Alexis, Addison, Avery, and Asher. Kim lost her eighteen-month fight with esophageal cancer in 2022 at age forty-seven.

In an example of God's amazing grace, he remarried in 2023 to Jessica. As widow and widower, they found love again, thanks to God's amazing provision. They live in San Tan Valley, Arizona, with Joe's three youngest children and Jeremiah, Jessica's son (who Joe calls his bonus kid and who calls him Papa Joe), in addition to their two bulldogs, two corgis, and a mutt named Diesel.

Joe and Jessica serve their church as members of the marriage leadership team and the prayer ministry. Jessica serves on the women's leadership team and in children's ministry. Joe is a leader at youth group and ushers on Sunday mornings.

You can find Joe's blog, The Bearded Dad, on Facebook.

Jordan Ramos was born and raised in Estes Park, Colorado. During her twenties, she lived in Guatemala, where she met and married her husband, Marlon. They have two beautiful children and currently reside in Colorado.

Jordan has a passion for traveling, learning about other cultures, and offering a helping hand. While living in third-world countries, several themes stood out, three of which were: people who had less were the most joyful, community is the strongest of foundations, and serving others reaps the highest blessings.

Jordan is currently writing *Connection*, a teen devotional journal with the goal of shining light on truth and encouraging a stronger connection with the Holy Spirit. The Lord's teachings will fill the pages, as Jordan is simply the one typing. The publication goal for *Connection* is the end of 2025, and the book will be found on Amazon.

Kirsten Wegele has always loved storytelling. It's something that God has flourished in her over the years, and she believes there is an importance in first telling your story. Over the years, she has learned that testimony is a huge part of who she is. Once Kirsten felt God had given her permission, she shared her testimony freely.

Kirsten is a lover of Jesus and passionate about being an open book to share her struggles, hurts, pains, losses, and faith with others for His Kingdom. She grew up in Highlands Ranch, Colorado, and has landed in a small farming town in Northern Colorado with her husband. They have seven children, three on this earth and four in Heaven.

In what the enemy meant for evil, God has truly worked for good in the lives of Kirsten and her husband. Some of life's toughest moments over the years have become catalysts of His greatness, healing, and love. God has truly changed her family to worship together, press *into* Him, and believe for more of His Kingdom to come!